KINGFISHER READERS

level **2**

Your Body

Brenda Stones

First published 2012 by Kingfisher
an imprint of Macmillan Children's Books
a division of Macmillan Publishers Limited
20 New Wharf Road, London N1 9RR
Basingstoke and Oxford
Associated companies throughout the world
www.panmacmillan.com

Series editor: Heather Morris
Literacy consultant: Hilary Horton
Commissioned photography by Howard Davies

ISBN: 978-0-7534-3056-9
Copyright © Macmillan Publishers Ltd 2012

9 8 7 6 5 4 3 2 1

1TR/1011/WKT/UNTD/105MA

A CIP catalogue record for this book is available from
the British Library.

Printed in China

Picture credits
The Publisher would like to thank the following for permission to reproduce their material.
Every care has been taken to trace copyright holders. However, if there have been unintentional
omissions or failure to trace copyright holders, we apologize and will, if informed, endeavour
to make corrections in any future edition
(t = top, c = centre, r = right, l = left):
Cover Howard Davies; pages 9t Shutterstock/Greenland; 9b Shutterstock/Andreas Gradin;
16b Shutterstock/Sebastian Kaulitzki; 17t Shutterstock/xjbxjhxm123; 19b Shutterstock/X.D. Luo;
25t Photofusion/Brian Mitchell; 25b Photofusion/Paula Solloway; 28t Shutterstock/Ramona Helm;
28–29 Shutterstock/Rob Marmion; 29t Shutterstock/Anyka; 31b Shutterstock/Rob Marmion; all other
photographs are by Howard Davies.

With special thanks to the following children for taking part in this book:
Jamie Andrews, Finley Chesson, Joe Chesson, Freya Cook, Joe Davies, Joe Dixon Bowley,
Ayobami James, Lena Hannigan, Sophia Ritchie and Libbi Walsh.

Contents

Outside and inside

You can see the outside of your body. You have arms and legs, called limbs. You have eyes and ears, called **organs**. Skin and hair covers your body.

But you can't see the inside of your body.

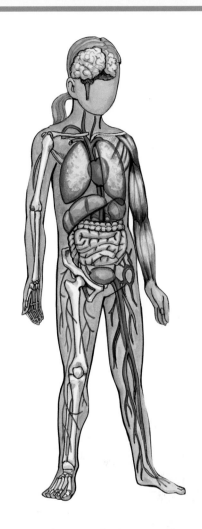

It has lots of pipes and tubes. Some carry air, some carry blood, and some carry food.

Arms

What do you use your arms for?

You use your arms for lifting and reaching, for pushing and pulling, for throwing and hanging.

Hands

What do you use your hands for?

You use your hands for washing
and brushing, for picking things
up and putting things down, for
writing and drawing.

Legs

What do you use your legs for?

You use your legs for walking and running, for jumping and swimming, for crouching and kneeling.

Feet

What do you use
your feet for?

You use your feet
for standing and
balancing, for
walking and
running, for
kicking and climbing.

Eyes

What do you use
your eyes for?

You use your eyes
for seeing. They
make tears when
you are sad.
They close when
you sleep.

Eyes can be
blue or brown
or green
or grey.

Ears

What do you use
your ears for?

You use your ears for hearing.
You hear loud and quiet sounds,
high and low sounds.

Your ears have wax inside to
trap dirt.

Nose

What do you use your nose for?

You use your nose for smelling nice and nasty smells, for **breathing** in and breathing out. Your nose is damp inside to help clean the air you breathe.

Mouth

What do you use
your mouth for?

Your mouth is for eating.
You taste food with your tongue.
You chew food with your teeth.

You use your mouth to talk,
smile and laugh.

Skin

Why do you have skin?

You have skin to cover and protect your body. Skin helps you touch and feel things. Skin also helps you keep warm and cool down. Skin can be different colours.

Hair

Why do you have hair?

Hair helps to keep you warm.
Hair can be different colours.
It can be long or short, curly or
straight. You have about 100,000
hairs on your head.

Bones

What is inside your body?

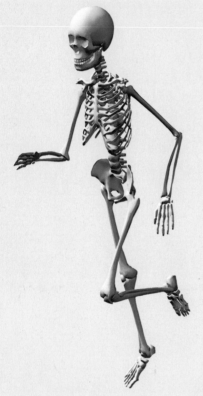

Bones make the shape of your body. Your bones make up your **skeleton**.

Everyone has 206 bones in their body. Half of them are the tiny bones in your hands and feet.

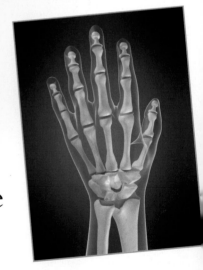

Muscles

What do muscles do?

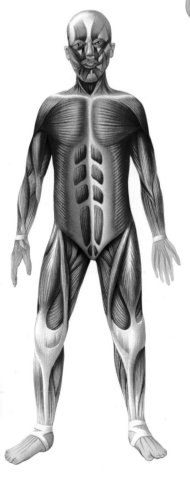

Muscles help you move your bones. They are like **levers** that pull your bones up and down. You have 650 muscles in your body. Your brain tells your muscles when to move.

Brain

Your brain is like a computer that runs your whole body. Each bit of your brain does a different job. It sends messages around your body and gets information back.

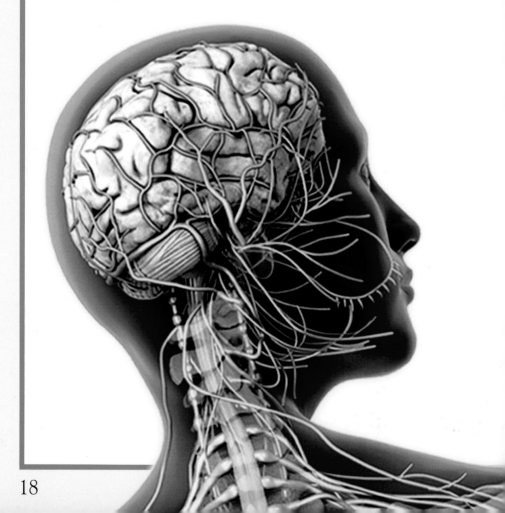

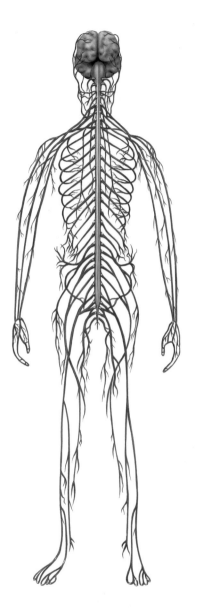

Nerves

Messages from your brain go down your nerves. Nerves are like thin wires. They link every part of your body to your brain.

If you touch something sharp, your nerves tell you to stop!

Lungs

You need to breathe air to live. Fresh air goes up your nose or mouth and down to your **lungs**. You breathe the old air out of your nose or mouth.

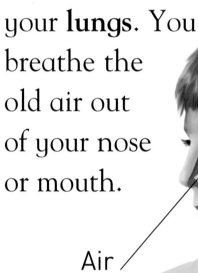

Air

Lungs

Blood

Blood runs all
round your body
in tubes. It carries
air from your
lungs and **energy**
from food to your
whole body.

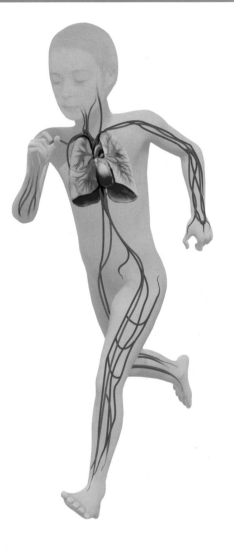

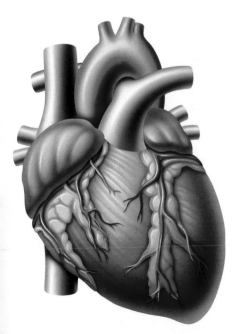

Your **heart**
pumps blood
round your
body.

Stomach

You eat food to give you energy.
You chew it with your teeth.
Then the little bits go down
to your stomach.

Your stomach breaks the
food down even more and
mixes it all up.

Digestion

After your stomach, the food goes to your **intestines**. This is where your body takes out the good parts to give you energy.

The waste comes out of your bottom when you go to the toilet.

Stomach

Intestines

Different bodies

Some of us are tall, some of us are short, some of us have different body shapes.

Some people can't walk and
need a wheelchair. Some can't
see or hear very well. We are all
different. That's what makes us
so interesting!

These girls
are using
sign language
to talk.

Keeping clean and fit

You have to look after your body to make it work well. Your body needs lots of exercise. It also needs lots of rest.

Make a plan
for looking after yourself.

- Take lots of exercise.
- Sleep 10 hours every night.
- Eat the right things.
- Clean your teeth twice a day.
- Wash your hands after going
  to the toilet and before eating.

If you get ill

Sometimes you get ill. You may get a headache or tummy ache. You may catch an illness, like a cold or flu.

Sometimes you have an accident and hurt yourself. You may have to go to hospital.

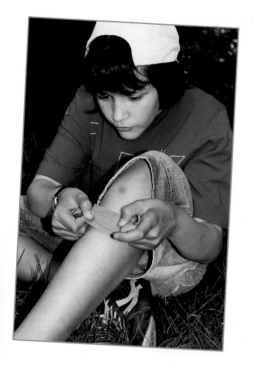

Sometimes you need to take some medicine or put on a plaster. Your body is very good at healing itself.

If you rest, lots of things get better by themselves.

Growing

You are growing very fast! Your hair grows 1 centimetre a month. Your fingernails grow five times as fast as your toenails. Your skin grows thousands of new **cells** every day.

Learning

Inside your body you are growing too. You are learning new words to say. You are learning new 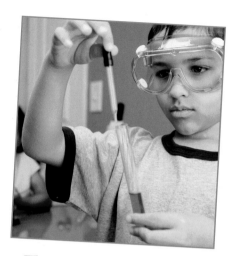 facts and new skills. Every year your brain grows bigger!

Glossary

breathing bringing air in and out of your body through your lungs

cells the smallest units that make up each part of your body

energy the power you get from food, which drives your body

heart an organ that pumps blood around your body

intestines organs that take out the good parts of your food

levers things that help to lift things

lungs organs in your chest that pump air in and out

organs parts of your body that do special jobs, like ears and eyes

skeleton the bones that make up your body